Our Lady of Guadalupe

Our Lady of Guadalupe

A New Interpretation of the Story, Apparitions, and Image

José Luis Guerrero

Liguori

Imprimi Potest:
Thomas D. Picton, CSsR
Provincial, Denver Province
The Redemptorists

Imprimatur:
Most Reverend Robert J. Hermann
Auxiliary Bishop
Archdiocese of St. Louis

Liguori Publications, a nonprofit corporation, is an apostolate
of the Redemptorists. To learn more about the Redemptorists,
visit Redemptorists.com.

To order, call 800-325-9521, or visit liguori.org

Contents

Prologue

Almost five centuries ago it happened, on December 12, 1531,
in the heart of the ancient city of México-Tenochtitlan. In the
presence of Bishop-elect Fray Juan de Zumárraga, an image of the
Virgin Mary was imprinted on the cloak *(tilma)* of Juan Diego
Cuauhtlatoatzin. That event, which seemed confined to a small
area in Mexico, was to have vast and profound consequences for
the entire American continent. Pope John Paul II recognized this
when he named the Blessed Virgin Mary patroness of all America
and canonized Juan Diego.

Why is this event still so important?

We are fortunate to have a written account of the events of
December 12, 1531, in a work titled *Nican Mopohua* by Antonio
Valeriano. The title *Nican Mopohua* comes from the work's
first two Aztec words, which mean "here is told, is set down in
order." It's not easy for us to grasp what it meant for those who
experienced the apparitions, but a new
translation can help understand their
implications for us today.

What follows is a recent translation
of the *Nican Mopohua* accompanied
by commentary that will enable us to
understand and live the message of our
Mother of Guadalupe.

Nican Mopohua
"Here is told,
is set down in order..."

Introduction

Here is told, is set down in order, how in a marvelous way the love of the Holy Virgin Mary, our Queen and the Mother of God, became visible there on Tepeyac, known today as Guadalupe.

At the first, she graciously permitted a humble Indian, Juan Diego, to see her, and in the end, in the presence of the recently appointed Bishop Don Fray Juan de Zumárraga, her love gave us her precious and beloved image.

Background

Ten years after the conquest of the city of Mexico, when arrows and shields were laid down, when everywhere on the mountains and the waters there was peace, there sprouted forth first the branch, then the blossoms. There came the truth, the knowledge of the One who is the source of all life: the true God.

The text begins by saying "when arrows and shields were laid down, when everywhere on the mountains and the waters there was peace." For the inhabitants of Mexico, war had been both their life and their religion. This was especially so for the Aztecs, who believed that through warfare they collaborated with their supreme deity, supplying human blood and hearts to maintain the harmony of the universe.

The idea that the universe could go on as before even though war had ended stripped the Aztecs of their very reason for existence and made them question the validity of everything they had previously done and believed. Thus, peace "on the mountains and the waters" was not something pleasant. It was just the opposite: the peace of a graveyard.

Moreover, Mexico City, which had dominated all the other cities, had been successfully conquered and destroyed. The battle for the city had not only been a fight between Spaniards and American Indians; it also pitted Indians against Indians, both for and against the Spaniards. In fact, the *conquistadores*—the conquerors—could have done nothing without their Indian allies. Thus, in one sense, the Indians were the true conquistadores. The Aztecs had been defeated and almost exterminated. The others were victors for at least a short time; however, their victories did not bring them glory, pride, or satisfaction. Rather, the victory of the combined Spanish and Indian force left the Indian "losers" thinking their whole culture and religion were useless. It seemed everything they had known and loved was condemned by God, and they had to forsake it all.

To properly appreciate the interpretation of the Guadalupe event, readers of *Nican Mopohua* must understand the author's use of botanical verbs such as *sprout* and *blossom* to express faith in "the truth, the knowledge of the One who is the source of all life: the true God." Metaphors from the plant kingdom expressed the highest human values for the indigenous; for them, "truth" was *nelliliztli*, meaning "rootedness" or "to take root." Only that which had a strong root was true. Although the root is the base, support, and foundation of every good plant, it cannot be seen because it is buried in the earth.

A beautiful flower is a witness to a plant's good and healthy root as well as a promise of its ability to bear good fruit.

It happened, then, in the year 1531, in a few days in the month of December, that there was a poor but honorable Indian gentleman named Juan Diego. It was said he owned houses in Cuautitlán, which belongs to the parish of Tlaltelolco.

It was exactly "in the year 1531." Indigenous people believed the date of a birth or of the beginning of some sort of program indicated that God is at work. The day on which the Blessed Mother left us her image, even though designated as December 12, 1531, was really December 22 because the European calendar was off by ten days. With the arrival of the winter solstice on December 21/22, the days gain more sunlight and begin to overcome darkness. The occurrence of the Guadalupe event thus had more importance for men and women who considered themselves the "People of the Sun." Moreover, the year 1531 was the turn of the century, from the fourth Mexican century to the fifth. (A Mexican century was equal to 104 European years. Mexican history begins in the year 1115, when Aztecs were supposed to have left Aztlán, their mythical place of origin.) In a culture that paid attention to numbers, the year 1531 was significant.

Cuautitlán, where Juan Diego owned houses, was not part of México-Tenochtitlan, and the inhabitants of Cuautitlán had joined with the Spaniards to fight the Aztecs. Thus, Juan Diego was not a conquered person, but a conqueror. Cuautitlán is rather far from Tlaltelolco. The text does not say Juan Diego *lived* in Cuautitlán at that time, only that he had houses there. Thus it is possible that he customarily lived in Tulpetlac. Nor does the text say Juan Diego was a poor man, contrary to popular opinion. It is more correct to present him as an Indian gentleman, a poor but worthy man, as so many of our indigenous brothers and sisters continue to be.

Juan Diego is described as a good Indian, which meant he possessed a solid Christian foundation. From their childhood, all Indians were taught by the missionaries to believe God loved them and that they had to respond to that love.[1]

First Apparition

It was Saturday, very early in the morning, when he went in search of the knowledge of God and of His commandments. As he drew near to the hill called Tepeyac, day was just dawning. He heard singing on the hill above, like the song of numerous fine song birds. When their voices fell silent, it seemed like the hill itself answered them,

in a most gentle and pleasing way; their songs surpassed those of the coyoltótotl *bird and of the* tzinitzcan *bird and of other fine song birds.*

The event begins as dawn is breaking; night is giving way to a new day. In the world view of native peoples, the night was the origin of all that is great and good rather than something fearful. Juan Diego was not on his way to Sunday Mass, but to the Saturday Mass in honor of Our Lady. When, over a century later in 1666, a formal hearing was convened to ascertain the truth of all that had taken place, the witnesses affirmed that "they called Juan Diego the pilgrim" due to those lengthy walks undertaken purely from devotion to Our Lady.[2]

In every culture, people have valued hills as places where men and women can get closer to the heavens and commune with the divine. Tepeyac is such a place, and it dominates the entire Valley of Mexico. Known to the Aztec people as the place where the temple of the mother goddess had previously stood, Tepeyac was deeply loved by the Mexican people. Therefore, the Blessed Virgin could not have chosen a better place to show them her love.

In pre-Hispanic poems, mountains are places where men and women meet God, offering him flowers as a gift of themselves. Indigenous people also loved music and dance. Songs (*In xóchitl in cuícatl*) were another way to communicate with God, the origin of all that is good. The singing of birds was a clear sign of God's presence. Although the Indians considered the presence of beautiful birds important, it was the beauty of the feathers that they thought a divine sign. The expression "jade and precious feathers" (*In chalchihuitl in quetzalli*) was for the Indians not only a symbol of beauty, but Beauty itself, meaning God. They also called a beautiful feather *Teocehualli*—the "Shadow of God."

Juan Diego stopped to see this thing. He said to himself, "Is there any chance I am worthy of this? Perhaps I am only dreaming. Am I asleep and only imagining? Where am I? What am I seeing? Am I perhaps in the place spoken of by our ancestors, the ancient ones? In that flowered land, the land of our sustenance, the heavenly land?

To Mexican Indians, those allusions to sleep indicate communication with the Divine and with their ancestors, who to played a very important role in their lives. At that time, missionaries believed the Indians had brought condemnation on themselves by serving idols, because the idols were really demons. Juan Diego begins to perceive that his Christian faith does not conflict with his ancestral religion.

He will not need to *destroy* what he and his ancestors had always venerated, but to *purify* it.

He fixed his gaze on the hilltop, toward the direction of the rising sun, because there also was the direction of the marvelous celestial song.

The text states that the sun *(Tonatiuh)* and "the marvelous celestial song" came from the same direction, joining the image of the rising sun with Jesus Christ, who rose from the dead.

And when the song had suddenly ceased, when it was no longer heard, then he heard that he was being called from the peak of the hill; that someone was calling him to come up, saying: "My dear Juantzin, *my dear* Juan Diegotzin."

Juan Diego knew the woman was Christian because she did not use his former name of Cuauhtlatoatzin, but his Christian name. And he knew the woman loved and respected him because she used the ending *tzin*, a reverential word that today's Mexicans express as a diminutive form.

One of the most important details of inculturation found in the narrative: it is not Jesus who comes to bring to completion the work of salvation, but the Blessed Virgin Mary, a woman. Today it is perfectly normal for women to take an active part in the apostolic life of the Church, but in the sixteenth century, almost five hundred years ago, there had never been even one female evangelizer; all were men. Women religious were permitted to take vows as contemplative nuns and pray behind the walls of a convent, but they were not allowed to directly participate in the apostolate.

The importance of the maternal figure in Mexico developed because there was a notably smaller number of men than women. With the pre-Hispanic Indian cultural attitude that war was necessary for religion to prosper, many of the men died young on the battlefield or as sacrificial victims. A boy grew up experiencing love and authority not so much from his father as from his mother. Mothers were tender and loving, but they were also very demanding and forceful, as was fitting for a warrior society. Thus, the maternal language of great tenderness was also one of authority and even of rigor. God knew very well that for Mexico, a female apostle, a *Mother* apostle, was essential.

Then in that very moment, there sprang alive in him a longing to go there, to the place from where he was called. He felt no fear, and in fact was brimming with happiness. So he began climbing the hill, going to see the place of the call.

The text emphasizes both the absence of fear and the presence of joy in Juan Diego's experience: he was totally happy and at ease. The Mexicans did not fear God, and they were convinced they were God's collaborators. They did not experience their religion, which was their life, as something terrifying, but as an ongoing celebration.

Arriving at the top of the hill, he was delighted to see a young woman, who out of love for him was standing, graciously inviting him to come closer. And when he arrived in her delightful presence he marveled at how her wondrous majesty surpassed all praises: Her garments shone like the sun, and the very rock upon which she stood seemed to emit beams of light. Her aura was as of a precious jewel, like jade, and the very earth seemed to ripple in splendor, shining like a rainbow in the mist. And the plants seemed like emeralds, their leaves the finest turquoise, their trunks, branches and thorns sparkling like gold.

Juan Diego encounters a young woman who is not only strikingly beautiful, but arrayed with "garments [that] shone like the sun," "Her aura a...precious jewel, like jade," "the very earth...shining like a rainbow," "plants...like emeralds,...turquoise, [and]...gold." These are symbols that, in a pre-Hispanic culture, denoted a divine nature. Far from being haughty or despotic, she waits for him, not seated on a throne as befits a queen, but standing; she calls him to come close beside her.

He bowed low before her, listening to her words. Loving and infinitely gracious they were, yet majestic and fascinating, as from a love to which all must yield. She said to him, "Listen, my dearest son, my Juan. Where are you going?"

And he answered her, "My Lady, my Queen, I go to your beloved house in Mexico Tlaltelolco. I seek the things of God that are given to us, taught to us by the priests, who are images of our Lord."

Juan Diego immediately identifies her; even before she introduces herself as the Mother of God, he associates her with his Christian religion, calling the church "your beloved house," where he is headed to "seek the things of God." He considers the Spanish Friars to be "images of our Lord." In a Náhuatl context, image was not only a representation, but something like "another self."

Right away, after this dialog with him, she made known her precious

will to him, she told him: "Know, and be assured, my dearest son, that I am the Perfect Ever Virgin, Holy Mary, the Mother of the one true God, of Ipalnemohuani (the One through whom all live), of Teyocoyani (the Creator of human beings), of Tloque Nahuaque (the Lord of nearness and closeness), of Ilhuicahua Tlaltipaque (the Lord of Heaven and of Earth). I greatly desire that my beloved sacred house should be built here, in order there to show Him to you all, to exalt Him, to present Him to the peoples, He who is all my love, He who is my compassionate gaze, He who is my help, He who is my salvation."

Juan Diego hears that the Christian Mother of God is also the Mexican Mother of God. The indigenous people of pre-Hispanic Mexico believed in a single God; the other "gods" were only appearances of the One, but this one God was considered too important to deal with directly. In Juan Diego's story, though, they hear that the one God loved them so much that he became like them through a human mother. Mary tells them that her Son is precisely Ipalnemohuani, Teyocoyani, Tloque Nahuaque, and Ilhuicahua Tlaltipaque, names which were unmistakable to them. The Lady, moreover, indicates that she greatly desires a temple in which she might show Jesus to them. The Aztec identity was strongly identified with their temple. Because the Aztec temples were gone, their nation had ceased to exist. Now that Mary requests a temple for her Son, the nation will rise again.

Next, she tells them she is also the mother of all of them. The "compassionate gaze" refers to her Son and to how she in her image looks at us.

"Because I am truly honored to be the compassionate Mother of all, both you and all the peoples here in this land, and still others who are my beloved, who call to me, seeking me, those who honor me, trusting in my intercession."

People with a hunger for God could hear nothing more beautiful. The Mother of God was honored to be their mother, "both you and all the peoples here in this land, and still others who are my beloved." This message involved an immediate and difficult requirement: accepting as their brothers and sisters not only all those who were in their own land, but all "others who are my beloved" as well. There had always been battles between groups, and now they were informed that they had a mother in common. Thus the *whole land* was her home, and she governed it. All of the peoples, including the Spaniards, were her children, which made them all brothers and sisters. Mary does nothing more here than repeat what her Son had requested in his high-priestly prayer: "Father...they may be one just as we are" (John 17:11). That was also the same ideal held by the pre-Hispanic peoples: everyone, even one's enemies, forms part of a group that must protect and safeguard itself. It was their idea of family as well: *cencalli,* which means "the whole house." Everyone who is in my mother's house is thereby part of my family.

"For there I am always ready to hear their cries and sadness, in order to purify and heal their sufferings and sorrows."

This is the perfect definition of a mother: one who is able "to hear their cries...purify and heal their sufferings and sorrows." One might ask, "Why console us when she could have kept us from having those same hardships, pains, and sorrows in the first place?" The answer is simple: no mother who truly loves her children keeps suffering and sorrow from them. These things are a part of life, and a mother knows that it is by passing through them that her children learn, progress, and grow.

Many tyrants and demagogues of history have promised they would eliminate the wretchedness, pains, and sorrows of their followers, offering instead a perfect world that is free of all attachments. Christ, much to the contrary, said that to "deny themselves and take up their cross and follow me" (see Matthew 16:24) was essential for his followers but that none who sought refuge in him would feel overwhelmed because "my yoke is easy, and my burden light" (Matthew 11:30). Mary of Guadalupe does the same thing.

"In order to accomplish that which He seeks, I pray that you will accept and go to the palace of the Bishop of Mexico. Tell him I myself send you as my representative to convey to him the great desire I have that he raise up for me in this place a sanctuary. Everything I will tell you, with all the details, you will tell him: all you have seen and heard."

It would have been very easy to ask Juan Diego to build a temple with the help of his friends. That temple, though, would not have been the cause of unity, but of division among the peoples, because the Spaniards would not have permitted it. Even if they had, it would have been an Indian temple, not a temple of and for all the peoples who are one in the land. Blessed Mary, the Mother of God, is not a goddess, she is a creature, and she gives us an example of honesty, instructing Juan Diego that "Everything I will tell you, with all the details, you will tell him: all you have seen and heard."

But Bishop Fray Juan de Zumárraga was not going to be easy to convince. Zumárraga was extremely proper even though he had something of a violent temperament. He was a distrustful inquisitor, in no way gullible and no sympathizer of images and popular devotions. His attitude toward the Indian religion was one of total rejection. In June 1531, barely five months before receiving Juan Diego in audience, he boasted in a letter to the general chapter of his order in Tolosa (Spain) of having destroyed as far as he could "five hundred temples of their gods and more than 20,000 images of the demons that they adored...." Adding insult to injury, he was not yet ordained a bishop. But he was someone who represented Christ on earth. He was, therefore, someone to whom Mary deferred. Even though he was not going to be easy to convince, she required that Juan Diego hide nothing from him. Truly, doing what Mary asked was not going to be easy.

"And be certain that I will be grateful to you and repay you for it. I will enrich you and exalt you. And you will greatly deserve my rewards for your weariness and your trouble in carrying out the mission I give you.

"Now you have heard my word, my beloved son. God grant that you go and be so good as to do all that is in your power."

The Virgin was not able to fulfill her promise to enrich Juan Diego materially because he later renounced even the little he had, dedicating the rest of his life to being the unpaid caretaker of her shrine. However, she did fulfill her promise in the sense that his fame was immediate, because Juan Diego and his uncle entered into history as very good Indians and very good Christians. All honors were dependent upon merits, being reserved always for the best qualified.

First Interview With Zumárraga

He promptly bowed in her presence and said, "My Lady, of course I go now to put to action your beloved word. And now I, your humble servant, take my leave."

Immediately he went down to put his mission into action. He took the direct road to Mexico, and arriving at the central part of the city, he went directly to the palace of the Bishop. The bishop— newly arrived in Mexico—was Don Fray Juan de Zumárraga, a priest of the Order of St. Francis.

Juan Diego obeys instantly and goes directly to see the Lord Bishop. On the Bishop's arrival in Mexico barely three years earlier, he had endured problems with the authorities of the first government group.

They kept him from communicating with Spain to prevent him from accusing them, and they had slandered him, denouncing him as a traitor at court. The court had summoned him to explain. Preoccupied with his imminent return to Spain to answer the charges, the Bishop would find Juan Diego to be an unnecessary distraction.

Upon arriving, Juan Diego sought immediately to see the Bishop, begging his servants to announce him. Only after a long time of waiting did they call him, after the Lord Bishop told him to enter.

When Juan Diego entered, he immediately knelt down, bowing low in the presence of the Bishop, and declared to him the message of the Queen of Heaven. He respectfully told him all the things he had seen and heard.

When he heard Juan Diego's message, the Bishop did not seem to believe him. He said to him, "My son, come back another time, when I will more carefully hear you. Then I will consider from the very beginning the reason you have come."

For any Christian of that time, much less a Spanish inquisitor, any story of a divine apparition having been seen by a recent convert would have provoked suspicion. But the appearance as described by Juan Diego, a telling heavily loaded with elements of his previous paganism—in which he asks for the construction of a temple to the Mother of God exactly where there had been the idol of the mother of the pagan gods Zumárraga had tried to demolish—would surely be viewed by Zumárraga as a satanic invention.

Second Apparition

Juan Diego left then, overcome with sadness because his mission was not immediately successful. He went straight back to the hill, and near day's end he arrived straight back at the hilltop. There, with great joy he met once again the Queen of Heaven. She was there, waiting for him, in the exact place where he had first seen her.

It takes little imagination to understand how wounded Juan Diego must have felt. If he had first seen the Virgin at dawn and now returned "near day's end," it was clear he had waited the better part of the day at the Bishop's residence. He must have felt exhausted and miserable about having to tell the Lady he had failed.

Upon seeing her, he bowed deeply in her presence, throwing himself on the ground. He said, "My Lady and my Queen, I went to where you sent me as your messenger. I went to carry out your word. Although it was very difficult, I entered the dwelling of the Chief Priest. I saw him, and in his presence I revealed your beloved word, as you sent me to do. He received me courteously and listened carefully, but from his answers, it appeared he was not convinced. He told me, 'Come back another time, when I will more carefully hear you. Then I will consider from the very beginning the reson you have come.'

"Clearly, from his response, he thinks the temple that you have given him the privilege of *building here is of my own imagining, and not from your own lips. Therefore, I beg of you, my Queen, my dear Child, that you send one of the nobles, a man respected and honored, to take your precious word, so that it may be believed. For, truly, I am nobody, a lowly man, a mere beast of burden. The place where you send me is no place for a man like me, my Lady. Please forgive me; I will only grieve your heart, falling into your just anger, O Lady."*

In this dialog we find various examples of refined graciousness, mixing formality and tenderness, solemnity and familiarity: "my Queen," "my Lady," "my dear Child."

Even though Juan Diego had spent his day waiting and being poorly treated, he describes his experience only with the polite euphemism "great difficulty." Juan Diego reasons that he cannot complain to the Lady without offending her because she was the one who sent him. Therefore, out of courtesy and deference he softens his report and attributes the failure to his own ineptitude, because any complaint would be seen as a reproach. In the same way, Juan Diego's politeness softens Zumárraga's insensitive reception.

It is important to remember this when Juan Diego seemingly tries to "fool her" by taking a different road to avoid meeting her. Nevertheless, he has a genuine interest in ensuring that the temple is built, so he begs her to send someone else, one who has the necessary qualities to get the task done.

The ever-glorious Virgin courteously answered, "Listen, my little one, know for certain that my servants are not few, messengers with whom I could send my word, who would carry out my will. However, it is imperative that you be the one, that it happen through your intervention. And I beg of you, my dear son, and I command you that tomorrow you go another time to see the Bishop. On my behalf, warn him, make him know clearly my will, that he construct the sanctuary that I ask. And once more, tell him it is no less than I, the Virgin Mary, the Mother of God, who sends you."

In the Gospel, Jesus insisted each of us is to be a worker in his harvest (Matthew 9:37; Luke 10:2), and that is exactly what the Blessed Virgin Mary does. She is also explicit that the evangelization of Mexico she seeks must be the work of everyone, both Indians and Spaniards. We have already seen that she requires the intervention of Zumárraga, but she is explicit in also requiring the same of Juan Diego. She rejects the implication that she is not familiar with the reality of Juan Diego, and that she is thus choosing an inept person. So she reiterates to him, in perfect agreement with Náhuatl etiquette, that "it is imperative that you be the one, that it happen through your intervention."

On the other hand, Mary's cordiality and tenderness doesn't belie her greatness: she is the Mother of God and can address Juan Diego, the Bishop and, indeed, the entire Church with the authority of a Queen: "On my behalf, warn him, make him know clearly my will, that he construct the sanctuary that I ask. And once more, tell him it is no less than I, the Virgin Mary, the Mother of God, who sends you."

And Juan Diego respectfully answered, "My Lady and my Queen, may I not afflict your heart with sadness. With great joy I will go and put to action your words. I will in no way fail, nor will I consider the way too difficult. I will go, but it may be that I will not be favorably heard, or if heard, not believed. However, tomorrow afternoon, as the sun sets, I will return to you with the response of the Bishop.

"Now I take my leave, my Lady, my Queen. Be at peace." And immediately, Juan Diego left for his house, to rest.

The Blessed Virgin Mary gave Juan Diego a difficult task by sending him back to the Bishop who had already rejected him. The task was dangerous, for the proposal to have a Christian church on the site of a pagan temple aroused suspicions of idolatry, which was punishable by death. When Moses received instruction to speak with the Pharaoh who had threatened to kill him, Moses used every excuse to avoid accepting (Exodus 4:1–13). So the contrast is notable, for Juan Diego answers the Blessed Virgin immediately: "With great joy

I will go and put to action your words. I will in no way fail, nor will I consider the way too difficult."

Second Interview With Zumárraga

The next day, Sunday, before dawn, while everything was still in darkness, he left his house, headed toward Tlaltelolco. He went to learn the things of God and to be counted in attendance. Then he went to see the Lord Bishop.

The reference "he left his house, headed toward Tlaltelolco" shows us that the text was written in Tlaltelolco. This confirms that its author was Antonio Valeriano, a student, teacher and rector of the Colegio de Santa Cruz established there.

At about ten in the morning, he was ready. He had heard Mass, was on the list, and the crowd had dispersed. So Juan Diego then went to the palace of the Lord Bishop. And as soon as he arrived, he did everything possible to have the privilege of seeing the Bishop. Finally, after much effort, he again received that honor.

He knelt at the feet of the Bishop, sad and weeping while explaining the will of the Queen of Heaven, hoping that in the end the message would be believed, that the Bishop would hear her instruction to build her sanctuary in the place she sought.

The previous day, Juan Diego had left immediately to fulfill the command of the Lady of Heaven, omitting even the Mass in her honor to which he was headed. Now, however, on Sunday, he does not consider himself exempt from attending Mass, nor does he appear before the Bishop as someone carrying an order reconfirmed by the Queen of Heaven. He comes with humility and fear, as someone who feels he could hinder something she desires: "He knelt at the feet of the Bishop, sad and weeping while explaining the will of the Queen of Heaven, hoping that in the end the message would be believed, that the Bishop would hear her instruction to build her sanctuary in the place she sought."

The Lord Bishop asked him many things, examining him, to be certain in his own heart. He asked Juan Diego where he had seen her and what she looked like. Juan Diego told the Bishop everything, in detail. Yet, despite the fact that every detail indicated that this was indeed the Virgin, the Mother of our Savior Jesus Christ, in the end her request was not obeyed. The Bishop said that the matter could not be done on the word of Juan Diego alone, but that some other sign was needed to know that, indeed, it was the Queen of Heaven who sent him.

The Lady had identified herself as the Mother of God, but she had not mentioned Jesus Christ. The identification of Jesus with Ipalnemohuani, Tloque Nahuaque, and Teyocoyani is due to Juan Diego, which shows the maturity and enlightenment of his faith, as well as the courtesy with which he had understood who it was who spoke to him.

Zumárraga was in no way gullible, and Juan Diego was hard-pressed: "The Lord Bishop asked him many things, examining him." Zumárraga was an inquisitor, an expert in interrogating people and in unmasking lies; he had been so harsh in doing so with the recently converted Indians that the Spanish Crown withdrew them from his jurisdiction. Still, Juan Diego passed the examination: "... every detail indicated that this was indeed the Virgin, the Mother of our Savior Jesus Christ."

Someone less demanding would perhaps have been satisfied with that, but Zumárraga was not. The examination could verify only that Juan Diego had not lied, which was insufficient reason to grant his request because Juan Diego could have had a hallucination. The Bishop, therefore, insists on proof, a sign, thus doing us an immense favor, because centuries later we still have the sign: the miraculous image we venerate still.

As soon as Juan Diego heard this, he said to the Bishop, "Ruling Lord, please choose what shall be the sign that you ask, since I will now leave to ask it of the Queen of Heaven, who sent me here as her messenger."

When the Bishop saw that Juan Diego confirmed everything without doubts or hesitation, he sent him off. But after he had left, the Bishop ordered some servants in whom he had confidence to follow, observing carefully Juan Diego's every move—where he went, whom he saw, and to whom he spoke.

That Juan Diego immediately accepted the request for a sign and, even more, his guileless question about what the sign ought to be, certainly had an impact on Zumárraga, for nothing disarms skepticism like evidence of good faith manifested by an openness toward inspection. But the Bishop was not convinced and ordered additional surveillance. In this he did not trust just anyone, but only "some servants, in whom he had confidence," giving them meticulous instructions: "…to follow, observing carefully Juan Diego's every move—where he went, whom he saw, and to whom he spoke."

And so they did. Juan Diego went straight out, taking the causeway. And they followed him, but there where the ravine comes out, at the wooden bridge near Tepeyac, he disappeared from sight. They searched everywhere but couldn't find him. So, furious at their failure, they turned back. They went back to the Lord Bishop, telling him that Juan Diego was not to be believed, that he was a liar, that he imagined everything that he had told the Bishop. And they decided among themselves that if Juan Diego returned, they would seize him and severely punish him to ensure that he would never again tell lies and stir up the people.

Their anger suggests that those trusted envoys had not thought all that highly of following Juan Diego. They thought it silly to give so much effort to someone so insignificant. That they lost sight of him does not necessarily imply something supernatural. It may have been the consequence of their own carelessness, which would simply increase their bad mood. In any case, despite their inability to testify to anything, they invent a "scapegoat" for their failure, deciding not only to slander Juan Diego as a liar, but if possible to assault him physically.

Third Apparition

During these events, Juan Diego was in the presence of the Holy Virgin, telling her the reply that he brought from the Bishop. And when he had finished, the Lady responded to him, "This is good, my beloved son. Tomorrow you will return here in order to take to the Bishop the proof, the sign he asked of you. With it, he will believe you and no longer doubt. And be certain, my dear son, that I will repay your care and the work and weariness you have done and endured for me. So now, go. Tomorrow, I await you."

Here things seem to change completely. Juan Diego's problems seemingly ended; he had successfully overcome the trials to which the Lady had submitted him. She calmed him, assuring him of the happy outcome of his mission; this must have given him great joy and a great desire to go back to harvest the fruits of that which she had asked him to sow so laboriously. But the worst was yet to come.

The Dying Uncle

But the next day, on Monday, when Juan Diego ought to have taken to the Bishop the sign that he might believe, he did not return. The reason was that when he arrived at his house, he found that his uncle, Juan Bernardino, was critically ill and near death. Juan Diego went searching for a doctor, but to no avail. At nightfall, his uncle begged him to go at daybreak to Tlaltelolco to call a priest, that he might come and hear his confession and prepare him for death. He was certain that it was the time and place of his death, and that he would not be healed.

In the Náhuatl culture, the "uncle" was a figure with no counterpart in modern society. With the real father frequently engaged in some distant war from which he might never return, someone always remained in charge of the family, looking after the wife and children: the "uncle." So for Juan Diego, his uncle was like his true father, someone with whom he had grown up and whom he loved the most.

We do not know what made Juan Bernardino sick, but we do know it was something unexpected. He had been healthy and well before Juan Diego left, and the illness struck suddenly, putting him at death's door in just a few hours. Nothing could be done, whether by himself or by the indigenous doctors to whom he had gone for assistance. This scenario suggests one of the plagues "imported" by the Spaniards. There was that year a plague of measles, and a plague of smallpox had claimed the lives of many Indians eleven years previously. This plague of measles was called *tepiton zahuatl*, "little leprosy."

The Indians had deep regard for the sacrament of reconciliation, and Juan Bernardino asks for "a priest, that he might come and hear his confession and prepare him for death" without mentioning either viaticum or anointing of the sick because initially these sacraments were not administered to the Indians.

Juan Diego puts aside things so immensely important and pleasing to him—like an appointment with the Mother of God and a mission to the Bishop, this time with an assured positive outcome—to care for his dying uncle. His pre-Hispanic culture had taught him that the sick are the image of God. His baptism would crown, not create, a solid virtue he already possessed.

So on Tuesday, still in the dark of the night, Juan Diego left from his house, going to Tlaltelolco to call a priest.

It is easy to imagine Juan Diego's discouragement, leaving his uncle in the middle of the night after a distressful and frustrating day, frozen half to death. He was going not to the glorious appointment with the Queen of Heaven, but to obtain a priest for his dying uncle. It is significant that, having to walk long hours in freezing temperatures (ice is mentioned in the narrative), he would not be wearing a small *tilma* hanging from his shoulders, as he is usually portrayed, but rather a *tilma* large enough to cover himself.

And when he came near the foot of the Tepeyac Hill, toward the place where the sun sets, the same place he had gone before, he said, "If I continue on the road, will the Lady not see me? And will she not, as before, stop me that I may take the sign to the Chief Priest, to confirm that she herself sent me? Please, first let our affliction leave us, that I might go quickly to call the priest. My uncle is waiting anxiously for him."

So he went around the hill, climbing a different part off to one side, toward where the sun rises, that he might quickly reach Mexico. He did not want to be delayed, even by the Queen of Heaven. He imagined that by going another route she would not be able to see him, she who out of love is always and everywhere watching us.

Juan Diego's actions seem foolish, imagining that "...by going another route she would not be able to see him, she who out of love is always and everywhere watching us." But it is only courtesy. It would never occur to him to demand a miracle as payment for his service. What matters most to him at that moment is providing his uncle with a confessor, and he rightly recognizes the importance of this task. He knows that he must refuse the Lady, and he does not want to cause her sorrow.

With his innate courtesy, a direct negative answer is unthinkably rude, so he does the same thing we Mexicans continue to do: he avoids directly saying no, sidestepping the obligation that cannot be met.

Juan Diego saw her, how she was coming down from the hilltop, from where she had been carefully watching him all the time. She came to meet him on the side of the hill, coming to block his way, and said to him, "What is it, my dearest son? Where are you going, and what are you going to see?"

Juan Diego, who knows nothing of the gift the Lady has for him, is troubled by her lack of courtesy. It was unthinkable that any well-educated person, much less a Queen, should have intercepted him, knowing he was purposely avoiding her because he could not grant that which she asked, and he didn't want to cause her distress. But the Lady, who shows she knows Mexican etiquette perfectly, understands well and is grateful for his maneuver, neither alluding to it nor insinuating the slightest annoyance or disapproval. Rather, she smoothes the way for Juan Diego, obliging him to open his heart to her: "What is it, my dearest son? Where are you going, and what are you going to see?"

And Juan Diego, was he perhaps a little ashamed, or a little afraid? Before her, he bowed and greeted her with great respect, saying, "My Virgin and my Queen, I pray you are content. How did you awaken this morning? Are you feeling well, my Lady? I fear I will bring sadness to your heart and face. Please know that a dear servant of yours—my uncle—is gravely ill, even on his death bed. A great disease has come upon him, such that he will surely soon die. Thus it is that now I must go urgently to your house in Mexico, to call one of the beloved of our Lord, a priest, so that he might hear the confession of my uncle, to prepare him. It is truly for this purpose we come into this world: to prepare for our death. But although I go to carry out this mission, as soon as I finish, I will immediately return here to carry your word, my Lady. Please forgive me and be patient with me. I am in no way deceiving you, my Princess, and tomorrow I will certainly and quickly return here."

Juan Diego's transparent honesty is admirable. He affirms his distress in not fulfilling his charge for her right away. He is hindered from doing so, he explains, by an even more important reason: the spiritual care of a dying person. It is the only thing he cannot postpone, he says, showing himself willing to disregard any other interest of his own. Rather, he promises her that "tomorrow I will certainly and quickly return here."

This is truly heroic, for he knows his uncle is on the verge of death. In fact, he is not sure the priest will reach his uncle in time; in the best of cases, his uncle will die shortly thereafter. So Juan Diego's offer to remain at the Lady's service the next day implied that he would not participate in the funeral of his beloved uncle. Although such participation was supremely important for every Indian, Juan Diego did not prefer it to his obedience of the Lady of Heaven.

As soon as she heard Juan Diego's words, she graciously responded, "Please pay attention to this, and may it be recorded in your heart, my beloved son. That thing that frightens and afflicts you is nothing. Do not let your heart be troubled. Don't fear this illness, nor any other form of illness or pain. Am I not here, I who am your Mother? Are you not under my shelter? Are you not held in my arms? Is there anything else you need? Now let nothing else disturb you, and do not be sorrowed by the illness of your esteemed uncle. He will by no means die now from this illness. I assure you that he is well even now." (And then, exactly at that time, she healed his uncle, as was later discovered.)

Juan Diego, upon hearing once more that the Mother of God was honored to be *his* mother, could not receive a better guarantee that he had nothing to fear. There was no one more loving and caring than an Indian mother. For Juan Diego, her tender words meant protection.

The Flowers

And Juan Diego, as he heard the beloved word of the Queen of Heaven, was greatly consoled by it. By it he had peace in his heart. He urgently requested that she immediately send him as a messenger to the Lord Bishop, to carry the sign of proof, that the Bishop might believe.

The Queen of Heaven then directed him to climb to the top of the hill, the place where he had first seen her. She told him, "Go up, my beloved son, up the hill, to where you first saw me and I instructed you. There you will see different kinds of flowers. Cut them, gather them together, and then bring them back down here. Bring them here before me."

Using flowers as proof of a divine command is original. In Europe, where flowers were merely for decoration and had no divine significance, this command would have made no sense.

As we mentioned, the Indian metaphor for truth, goodness, and the worth of a person was "to take root"; in other words, a thing is certain or good if it has good roots. A beautiful flower is evidence of good roots and a promise of good fruits. So our Indian ancestors loved flowers. There was nothing more beautiful, more divine, no more sublime a gift of God than flowers. Xochitlalpan ("the Land of Flowers") was paradise.

Considering that, we understand why Juan Diego trembled with happiness on hearing what the Lady asked of him.

Juan Diego quickly climbed the hill. Arriving at the top, he was astonished at the varieties of marvelous flowers, all in bloom with petals opened. It was not the season for them, and in truth it was the worst of the ice season. Yet, the fragrance of the flowers was strong, and droplets of dew covered them like pearls.

Quickly, he began cutting them, and, gathering them all together, he put them in the hollow of his poncho. Clearly, the top of the hill was not a place where flowers grew. The place had an abundance of rocks, thistles, cactus and mesquite—and ice. It was, after all, December, the time when ice destroys everything.

Juan Diego's joyful wonder is evident as he witnesses God's flowers blooming and opening their petals on Tepeyac Hill, a special marvel in the poor-quality terrain. The Valley of Mexico, although not very large (80 miles at maximum length), has always had notable contrasts, being humid with forested mountains in the south and parched and arid toward the north, where Tepeyac Hill is located. For Juan Diego, then, the flowering was the meeting of Omeyocan, the world of God, with Tlactípac, the world of man. This was evidenced by the transformation of the hill, rough and naturally sterile, into a garden that surpassed Tlalocan, the paradise of the god of water.

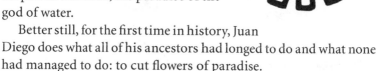

Better still, for the first time in history, Juan Diego does what all of his ancestors had longed to do and what none had managed to do: to cut flowers of paradise.

Juan Diego went quickly back down, taking to the Queen of Heaven the diverse flowers that he had cut. She took them in her hands and then arranged them, placing them again in the hollow of his poncho. Then she told him, "My dear son, these varied flowers are the proof, the sign that you will take to the Bishop; on my behalf you will say to him that he must see in them my wish, and that by this sign he must carry out my wish, my will. And you, you who are my messenger, in you I place absolutely all my trust; and I firmly instruct you that only in the presence of the Bishop shall you spread open your ayate, shall you show him what you bear. To him you will recount everything precisely, you will tell him that I directed you to climb to the top of the hill to cut the flowers, and each thing that you saw and marveled at, so that you may convince the Lord Bishop, so that he may immediately do what is within his power to build, to raise the sanctuary that I have requested."

The supreme proof of Indian courtesy and love for someone was to personally give flowers. When that could not be done, such as when the emperor had too many invited guests, only the most beloved of his people could give flowers on the emperor's behalf. So for the Lady to give flowers to Juan Diego and to entrust them to him, saying, "My dear son, these varied flowers are the proof, the sign that you will take to the Bishop," was a sign of high esteem. Yet she adds, "And you...are my messenger, and in you I place absolutely all my trust." She tells him again that he must deal only with the Bishop, telling him "each thing that you saw and marveled at."

And as soon as the Heavenly Queen gave him his commission, he set out on the causeway, he went straight to Mexico; and this time he went in high spirits. This time his heart was free from worry, because his mission would turn out well, because he would accomplish it perfectly. He went along, taking great care of what was in the folds of his garments, lest anything should fall out; he went along, taking great pleasure in the fragrance of the various precious flowers.

The deference of the Lady of Heaven toward the Bishop, by commanding that only to him should the flowers be given, emphasizes for the Indians that the flowers are the Bishop's and no one else's. Juan Diego would have liked to cry out to all within hearing. He would have liked to share with them the sublime marvel of these flowers that he bore in his *tilma*, but he did not do so; he went straight to Mexico.

Third Interview With Zumárraga

Upon Juan Diego's arrival at the Bishop's palace, the doorman and other servants of the Bishop came to meet him. Juan Diego begged them to tell the Bishop that he wished to see him, but they would not. None of them wanted to help him. In fact, they ignored him. Perhaps that was because it was still dark. Or perhaps because they already knew him, that he did nothing but bother them and cause them trouble. And surely their companions—the ones who had lost sight of him while following him—had already told them about him.

Here Juan Diego's faith, even though he has been assured of success, is brought back down to earth. When he arrives at the Bishop's palace, well before dawn, things begin as poorly as could be feared, for the servants would not let him in. Today, anyone coming to see the Archbishop of Mexico while it is still very dark out would rightly be considered tactless or disrespectful; the least one could expect is to have to wait awhile. But in those days, before electric lights, all were early risers. Thus, Zumárraga was almost certainly awake even before Juan Diego arrived and would not have had a problem receiving him early on.

During a very long period of time he was kept waiting for a reply. And when they saw that he had been there for such a long time, standing crestfallen, doing nothing, waiting to see if he would be called, and noticed how he seemed to be carrying something in the fold of his tilma, *they swiftly approached him to see what he carried and to humor themselves. When Juan Diego saw that it was impossible to hide from them what he carried, and that they would probably bully him, that they would likely throw him out or would perhaps rough him up, then he showed them just the littlest bit that they were flowers. And when they saw that they were all fine, varied flowers, and knowing that it was not the season for them, they marveled at them greatly: how fresh they were, how wide open their petals were, how fragrant they were, how beautiful they looked; and they coveted them, yearned to get hold of some of them, to run off with some of them. Three times they dared to grab the flowers, but they failed to do so, because each time they tried to take them they could no longer see flowers, but rather what seemed like something painted, or embroidered, or sewn on the* tilma.

The humility and fortitude Juan Diego displayed before those insolent servants was not fear, but the self-control of a refined person in the presence of fools, something he had learned from the time of his boyhood.

The failure of the servants' attempts to snatch the flowers could also seem like a legend, but it is not so. The necessity of that episode is to be found, first of all, in the fact that Juan Diego considered it sacrilegious for a stranger to touch the flowers of God. But it was even more important to make clear the singular right of the Spanish Bishop to receive those flowers before anyone else. This was confirmed for them when it was demonstrated that a supernatural force backed up his declaration that the Mother of God, when giving him those flowers, had categorically established: "I firmly instruct you that only in the presence of the Bishop shall you spread open your *ayate*, shall you show him what you bear." It was another way to endow the representative of her Son with indisputable authority. It also served to open the way for Juan Diego to see the Bishop.

With that, they went immediately to report to the Lord Bishop what they had seen, how a lowly Indian—the same who had come the other times—wanted to see the Bishop and had been waiting a very long while.

As soon as the Lord Bishop heard of this, it moved his heart: This was the proof that he might accept what this man had been telling him. And immediately he ordered that Juan Diego enter and come in to see him.

The strange event of the "untouchable" flowers immediately began to fulfill the promise of the Lady of a favorable change in the Bishop's attitude. The Bishop, who had accepted without question the negative reports of his servants, now receives Juan Diego without hesitation.

Juan Diego entered and bowed low before the Bishop, and once again respectfully told the Bishop the things he had seen and at which he had wondered. Once more, he gave him his message.

Juan Diego begins a detailed report about everything that had occurred, which gives us his own point of view. The first thing we notice is that, besides courtesy, Juan Diego demonstrates authentic virtue. He banishes from his narrative all traces of complaint or reproach, with no reference to his humiliations or his distress over his uncle's illness. He spells out only the interests of the Lady, the only thing that matters to him.

The Version of Juan Diego

With great respect, he said to him, "My Lord Bishop, I have done what you asked me to do. I took your request to the Lady, the Queen of Heaven, telling her that you respectfully seek a sign, that you might believe me, that you might construct for her a beloved house there in the place she asked. I also told her that I had given you my word to bring to you a sign, proof of her will, as you have instructed me.

"She gladly heard your word and took pleasure in your request for a sign, some proof that you might carry out her will. And today, while it was still night, she sent me once again to see you. I asked her for something, some sign that I might be believed, and she said she would give me one. Then, in that very instant, she answered my request, sending me to the top of the hill, to the place where I had previously seen her. There, I was to cut a variety of beautiful flowers.

"And after I went to cut them, I brought them back down. Then with her own hands she took them and placed then again in the

hollow of my tilma. She did this that I might bring them to you, to present them personally to you.

Though I well knew that the hilltop was no place for flowers—it is a place of only rocks, thorns, cactus and thistles—I never doubted or hesitated. When I arrived at the top, I was astonished: It was paradise! Here there was gathered every sort of flower imaginable, blossoms of superb quality, shining with dew, such that I—overcome by emotion—began at once to cut them. And the Lady gave me the honor to bring them to you, which I now do, so that they might be to you the sign you seek that you might carry out her will, that the truth of my message may be evident. Here they are: Do me the honor of receiving them!"

A place "of only rocks, thorns, cactus and thistles," plants typically found in desert regions, was obviously not naturally compatible with those marvelous flowers, and even less so in the month of December when the ice devours everything. That Juan Diego had not doubted or hesitated is significant. That place where flowers were impossible was the place where Mexicans would most have wanted them: Tepeyac Hill. Because it was the mountain of the Mother Goddess, Tepeyac had a special affection for a nation so attached to the maternal image. Therefore, the destruction of that temple must have been especially painful. Now God had covered the hill with his own flowers, converted it into his Xochitlalpan, Tonacatlalpan, the place that our ancestors, our grandparents always told us about. This was the very best of the Good News they could hear.

Juan Diego is a likeable figure for all Mexicans, but few see him in his supernatural dimensions. For the great majority of Mexicans, he was an *indito*: a sort of big child, very good, guileless, courteous, humble—and that's all.

As the disposition of the chosen ones of God, faith has always counted decisively for obtaining his blessing (Matthew 8:10, 9:22,

15:28; Mark 10:52; Luke 7:9). The faith of a young Girl, the same Girl who came down to Tepeyac Hill, changed the history of the world: "Blessed are you among women, and blessed is the fruit of your womb. And how does this happen to me, that the mother of my Lord should come to me?...[B]lessed are you who believed... From now on will all ages call me blessed" (Luke 1:42, 43, 45, 48).

Inversely, lack of faith can lead to grave consequences: "But the LORD said to Moses and Aaron: 'Because you did not have confidence in me, to acknowledge my holiness before the Israelites, therefore you shall not lead this assembly into the land I have given them'" (Numbers 20:12).

The vocation God bestowed upon Juan Diego Cuauhtlatoatzin was in some aspects more difficult than the vocation he bestowed upon Moses, for it was even more revolutionary than leading a people to shake off oppression. Juan Diego's vocation had to do with the same thing Saint Paul proclaims about Christ Jesus: to achieve the impossible, to reconcile the irreconcilable. "For he is our peace, he who made both one, and broke down the dividing wall of enmity, through his flesh, abolishing the law with its commandments and legal claims, that he might create in himself one new person in place of the two, thus establishing peace, and might reconcile both with God, in one body, through the cross, putting that enmity to death by it" (Ephesians 2:14–16).

And so, for those with eyes of faith, Juan Diego is a benefactor— the true founder of Mexico, "Father of the Fatherland." His faith made Mexico a truly *mestiza* nation. His faith, fulfilling his mission as the bearer of flowers that imprinted an image, made this possible.

Fourth Apparition: The Image on the *Tilma*

And with that, standing up, he spread open his white tilma, in whose folds he carried the flowers. Thus as all the varied, precious flowers fell to the ground, at that very instant the Beloved Image of the Perfect Virgin, Holy Mary, Mother of God, became a sign, appeared

suddenly in the same form and figure as it now is, where it is now kept in her dearly beloved house, in her dear, sacred house at Tepeyac, which is called Guadalupe.

To make flowers spring forth on Tepeyac Hill was a clear sign for the Indians, but the image that appeared all of a sudden on the *tilma* of Juan Diego is even more so. The rough *ayate* of an impoverished Indian, used and worn out, was far from being a satisfactory cloth on which to do any sort of painting. It was inappropriate for its obvious technical unsuitability as well as for moral reasons. To strip a *poor* man of his poor clothes—clothes that also served as a tool of his work, useful for hauling things—to send a message to a *powerful* man, sounds at the very least like bad taste and at worst like exploitation.

Of course, it is likely that Juan Diego did not even think about that, and that any Mexican would have given all he possessed to honor a person of authority. But that does not justify the abuse of his generosity. On the contrary, his generosity imposes upon the authority an obligation to anticipate and seek to check it. And if that authority is God himself, we must agree—from the European point of view—that the gesture is in bad taste at the least. But for Juan Diego and all of his people, it was profoundly different: for him, the use of his *tilma* constituted an unimaginable honor.

That an image of the Mother of God should be sent to a people who communicated by using images was a perfect catechesis. And it was even more eloquent, because for the Indians the *tilma* also symbolized the person: matrimony was accomplished by tying together the man's *tilma* and the woman's *huipil*. Thus, with both image and *tilma* being "sacraments" of the person, the idea of fusing the two was an inspired adaptation to Indian culture.

In addition, this gesture resolved an unresolvable problem. The missionaries, in good faith, not only haggled over giving the Eucharist to the Indians and totally omitted the final anointing (extreme unction), they also excluded them from the priesthood and the religious life. This meant that the growth of the Church in Mexico was in danger of being halted, because Christ's Church is a communion of charity in which all are equals. That would take centuries to change. How, then, could God make clear to the Indians that in his eyes they were equal to the Spaniards—without denying or offending the Spaniards? For, though they were mistaken in these matters, the Spaniards were still his authentic spokespersons.

We see, then, that by commanding that her message and her sign be given only to the Bishop, Mary conferred upon the Bishop an immense prestige and authority. It made the Bishop the proprietor of her image. Further, Mary clearly told the Mexicans, in their own language, what she told the waiters in Cana of Galilee: "Do whatever he tells you" (John 2:5). That is, even though at times it may be difficult for them, everything the Bishop says is Mary's word. And, subordinate to the Bishop, she also exalted Juan Diego, whom she designated her *Teomana,* which means "Bearer of God of the New Kingdom." Because Juan Diego, whether by birth or by impoverishment, was a man of the people, it was clear his example was achievable by all.

To distinguish in that way, jointly and with genuine solidarity, a Spaniard and an Indian—and that particular Spaniard, the supreme religious authority, and that particular Indian, one of the lowly, one like so many others—"inculturated" the Scripture: "There is neither Jew nor Greek, there is neither slave nor free person, there is not male and female; for you are all one in Christ Jesus" (Galatians 3:28).

The image of Guadalupe has always been venerated, but from the first it has also been rigorously studied. We still have the image, we conserve it, and we can continue to study it more and with better analytical instruments. The image of Our Lady continues to astonish us, speaking to us five centuries later with the language that amazes and convinces us: the language of scientific analysis, because no scientist has hit on a plausible explanation for its preservation.

When the Lord Bishop, along with the others who were present, saw it, they fell to their knees in astonishment. Then they stood again to see it, profoundly moved and convinced in their hearts.

The Lord Bishop, with tears of remorse, begged her to pardon him for not having immediately carried out her will. Then he stood up and untied the neck of the garment of Juan Diego. On this garment had appeared the image of the Lady of Heaven, the sign, and with great respect, he removed it and carried it away to a place in his chapel. Juan Diego spent the entire day in the Bishop's house, at the insistence of the Bishop. And on the following day, he told him, "Let's go, so that you might show me the place where the will of the Queen of Heaven would have me build her a sanctuary." And immediately, people were invited to build it, raising it up.

Juan Diego remained "in the Bishop's house, at the insistence of the Bishop." This gesture by Zumárraga continues to indicate caution, even distrust; and for Juan Diego that must have been very hard. He had not told any of his own people what he had gone through; he had been away from home for two days without explanation, and he had heard nothing further about his uncle. He had left him on his deathbed, but he did have the Lady's promise of finding him alive—something he ardently sought to confirm. So obedience could not have been easy for him, but obey he did, and without a hint of anything different.

The Healed Uncle

Juan Diego, when he had pointed out where the Lady of Heaven had ordered that her sanctuary be built, asked permission: He wanted to go home to see his uncle Juan Bernardino, who had been in his bed and gravely ill when Juan Diego had left to summon a priest from Tlaltelolco to come and hear the confession. It was the same uncle whom the Queen of Heaven had told him was already healed.

But the others did not let him go alone, instead accompanying him to his house. Upon arriving, they saw his uncle without pain, healthy and content. And Juan Bernardino was surprised to see his nephew escorted and honored. He asked Juan Diego why he was so highly honored.

Juan Diego has returned to see his uncle after leaving him apparently dying early Tuesday morning, when Juan Diego had gone off to seek a confessor. And so, as soon as he points out the place for the church, he asks permission to withdraw, which he is granted. Yet, Zumárraga is not letting down his guard. It is important for the Bishop to know the truth: whether a dying man has been made suddenly and totally healthy. Therefore, he grants permission, but "the others did not let him go alone, instead accompanying him to his house." This was a ploy: the "honor" thus mitigating the control—something Zumárraga still does not relinquish. There was no doubt, and the uncle understands it this way, that Juan Diego was honored by his escort; but it is also apparent that with the honor came some control.

Zumárraga had spent a whole day with Juan Diego and had been won over by Juan Diego's candor and virtue. In fact, later the Bishop will let him live as the guardian of the shrine and receive holy Communion three times a week, something almost unheard of at that time. Despite this, Zumárraga maintains his guard and carries out his examination thoroughly.

Fifth Apparition:
The Name of Guadalupe

Juan Diego told his uncle that when he had gone out to call the priest for confession, there at Tepeyac the Lady of Heaven appeared to him. She sent him as her messenger to Mexico to see the Lord Bishop so that he might build her a house in Tepeyac. And she had the kindness to tell him not to be upset, that everything was well with his uncle. And with that he was at peace.

The uncle's surprise shows that he knew nothing, from which we learn that Juan Diego could be discreet. The only human being with whom he had spoken of the matter was the one with whom the Lady had commanded him to speak, the Bishop, even though she never forbade him to speak with others. To be discreet and diligent, to do everything one was told and more, was basic advice from parents to their children.

Juan Diego's uncle, Juan Bernardino, told him it was true, that at that precise moment she had healed him. And at that same time, he saw her in exactly the same form in which she had appeared to Juan Diego himself. Further, he told his uncle how she had also sent him to Mexico to see the Bishop, and when he saw the Bishop, he should inform him of every detail of what he had seen and the marvelous way she had healed him. Also, that she said that her precious image should be called and she should be known as The Eternal Virgin, Holy Mary of Guadalupe.

The intervention of the uncle, Juan Bernardino, is essential within the Guadalupe event because without this last apparition, the event would have been incomplete for everyone involved, especially Zumárraga. The flowers and image said little within the parameters of the Spaniard's culture, and he needed solid proof to give his support with a serene conscience. The instantaneous healing of a dying man, which Zumárraga scrupulously verified, provided the additional proof, independent and fully in agreement.

Upon the inquisitor's examination, this last apparition was found to be as valid as the first ones. With great courtesy, the Lady had yielded her place to the Bishop, commanding also that everything should be submitted to his judgment. She offered him a new element that entirely put to rest his suspicions: "She said that her precious image should be called and she should be known as The Eternal Virgin, Holy Mary of Guadalupe."

Here we need to emphasize another important feature that might otherwise pass unnoticed. The Blessed Virgin Mary conferred the great honor of revealing the name by which she wished to be invoked not to Juan Diego, but to his elderly uncle. This mirrors the Indian reverence for elders.

Now, *Guadalupe* is not a Spanish or Náhuatl word. Náhuatl lacks the consonants *G* and *D*. Rather, it is Arabic: *Wadi al Lub*, which means "River of Black Gravel." Further, *Guadalupe* does not seem to have been the original name. But it is understandable that God may have wished for the Arabic title of Guadalupe to become the very soul of that Mexico that was born with her. That is the title with which his Mother had been venerated for centuries as the Queen of Spain, the motherland of those who brought the faith to Mexico. There was nothing more appropriate for the one who declared herself "honored to be the compassionate Mother of all, both you and all the peoples here in this land, and still others who are my beloved, who call to me, seeking me, those who honor me" than to have a Jewish maiden with an Arabic name assimilated by Spain become the very soul of the American continent.

The Beginning of the Devotion

Quickly, they brought Juan Bernardino into the presence of the Lord Bishop, to speak these things and to give testimony before him. And together with his nephew Juan Diego, Juan Bernardino was lodged in the Bishop's house for some days, during the entire time the sanctuary of the Queen was being built there on Tepeyac, in the place she had shown herself to Juan Diego. And the Lord Bishop transferred to the Principal Church the precious image of the Child of Heaven. It seemed good to him to take it from his palace, his chapel where it had been, so that the entire population could see and admire this marvelous image.

No doubt bringing Juan Bernardino before Zumárraga resulted from specific instructions from the Bishop himself, so he could take an official declaration from the old man. Therefore the Bishop kept both uncle and nephew with him for several days. Once satisfied all was in order, "the Lord Bishop transferred to the Principal Church the precious image of the Child of Heaven...so that the entire population could see and admire this marvelous image."

Everyone in the city was excited at the opportunity, and crowds were gathering to see and admire the beloved image.

Let us attempt to do the same: "to see and admire the beloved image." The image is 143 centimeters high, and the present dimensions of the cloth are 1.75 x 1.05 meters: too high for the *tilma* to have been used as the short and loose cloak with which Juan Diego is normally portrayed in paintings.

The idea of using an *ayate* as a canvas for a picture presented a problem: *ayates* were woven by hand on waist looms. That meant they were necessarily narrow, so that to form a sufficiently large cloak, the *ayate* had to be made of at least two pieces sewn together with a coarse seam. To center two symmetrical human figures, the Virgin and the angel, would require splitting them in half. The figures are, in fact, at the center line of the cloth, yet the seam does not divide them. How was this done?

By having the Virgin turning toward her right with her head bent at a twelve-degree angle, also to her right, the seam does not touch either her face or hands and barely grazes the forehead of the angel, who is turned toward his left, thus balancing the inclination of the Virgin's head.

This produces a curious effect: geometrically, the volumes are equal on both sides yet, as we face the image, most of the image is on our left side. If the entire right side is covered, the image remains nearly intact: perfectly visible are the Virgin's face, neck, both hands with the embellishments of the cuffs, the ribbon at her waist, part of her cloak and almost all of her gown, plus one of the tips of the crescent moon and one foot. Also visible is the face and most of the body of the angel, of whom only one arm and one wing remain outside. In other words, nearly all of the image is on our left side; it is not really a frontal view, but rather a three-quarter profile.

If the left side is covered, it's impossible to tell who is depicted because neither face can be seen—just barely a bit of the cloak, gown, and moon as well as an arm and wing of the angel.

This creates an enormous visual disproportion. Nonetheless, the painter created his art in such an inspired way that it is not even noticeable, for the volumes are balanced by the distribution of their elements and of the light. The right side is much brighter than the left, to the degree that the smaller part of the gown seems larger because it is more brilliant and has many fewer pleats. The cloak occupies more space, and we see more of its interior. It is also a lighter shade and has more and larger pleats than the part on the left, which has none except on a very narrow knee-high band, where it perfectly balances the section on the left side. On the right side, the light interior is showier and the pleats are much fuller and larger.

At the height of the arms, an ample fold under the Virgin's left arm (our right side) visually compensates for the great bow of the cincture. It, in turn, is the only element on that side that presents abrupt angles, which abound on the left side. The most noticeable of these, at almost 90 degrees, is formed by the cloak over the gown with the fold that supports the Virgin's left forearm (our right side), and the rest which falls freely, both seen by the brighter, internal part. Facing the image, the right part of the moon is also noticeably larger than the left.

The inclination of the Virgin's head, which creates an empty spot in the upper right corner, is compensated for by a fold of the cloak hanging down in the lower left corner. This fold is of a noticeably different shade of blue, rather greenish and muted; on it, three stars rest comfortably. The imbalance this would create with the corresponding lower-right corner, where there is neither cloak nor foot, is compensated for by the greater size of the moon and an extension of the gown that not only juts out but is much brighter, and, above all, by the slightly raised knee, which is seemingly in the act of beginning a step forward. It could also be understood as a dance step in the minds of the Indians because, for them, to dance was nothing less than to create, the highest way to worship God—ultimate prayer.

Another important element is the face. In the Guadalupe event, there is not a word of scolding or rebuke. And yet there is a message of disapproval, hard and direct, although it is formulated with all the discretion of what is implicit in the face of the Heavenly Child, an unmistakably *mestizo* ("mixed-race") face. This is common in today's Mexico but was not then. At the beginning, this mixing of the races was enthusiastically accepted by the Indians, who gladly gave their daughters and sisters for marriage to the Spaniards. However, when the children of those unions were born, their fathers would abandon them, considering the mothers dishonored by having created *mestizo* children. The end result was that both groups, Spanish fathers and Indian mothers, rejected the fruit of their union, and a lower class composed of a great number of abandoned *mestizo* children came into being.

In both Mexico and Spain, children were—and are—deeply loved, so that the rejection and abandonment brought profound psychological damage that hurt parents and children alike. Therefore, although it was hard to accept a Blessed Virgin with the face of a *mestiza*, by showing both groups that what they perceived to be humiliating was, for her, something as precious as she was herself, the Blessed Virgin sent a sublime reiteration of her message of unity and transcendence.

Another visual "trick" is the sun, appearing behind the image, more brilliant at the height of her womb, seemingly blazing a trail through the mist. As previously mentioned, the mist would bring to the Indian mind the idea of *Mixtitlan Ayauhtitlan*, which means "amidst clouds and mist." This in turn would evoke the image of  the Virgin standing with her back to the rising sun. But given the strong frontal illumination and the angle of the shadows, especially the shadow on the Virgin's slightly raised left knee, it appears that the only source of that light is already higher than the horizon and that, given its position southeast of the winter solstice, the Virgin is really looking toward the northeast. This is a stroke of genius by the painter, because for Indian eyes it indicates in its totality that the Lady is divine. "She comes among clouds and mist" and is pregnant with the sun, but a sun different from the physical one, since the physical one is illuminating her from the front.

As is all of the Guadalupe event, the image is a synthesis of European and Mexican painting, which are intrinsically incompatible. The colors, the outlines that are accentuated, the golden arabesques painted on the gown without following its pleats, and the richness of its symbolism are all clearly Indian. The skill mastery of light, shadow, volume, and perspective would do honor to the greatest European painters.

In the Mexico of the first half of the sixteenth century and throughout all the centuries of its colonial paintings, it was a waste of time to seek someone capable of copying the image or even of tracing it, not to mention finding some genius capable of actually creating such a work.

An image so unique and beautiful, even from the mere aesthetic point of view, would both shake the Indians to their very foundations and hold a high interest for the Spaniards. Yet neither Zumárraga nor any Spaniard then could imagine an insignificant episode developing into the cornerstone of the Church's establishment in Mexico and the nucleus around which the very essence and history of the Mexican peoples would forge itself and gravitate.

The Conversion of Mexico

And absolutely all the inhabitants of the city, without exception, were profoundly moved when they came to see and marvel at her Precious Image. They came to recognize its divine nature. They came to present their prayers to her. Many of them marveled at the miraculous way it had appeared, since absolutely no one on earth painted her Beloved Image.

At the end of 1531 there were in all of Mexico barely a handful of missionaries who knew the indigenous languages; no one yet had a genuine command of them. And yet, beginning in 1532, the Indians presented themselves to the missionaries in great numbers, spontaneously asking for baptism. What had happened? The Queen of Heaven had shown them that she had not "come to abolish the law or the prophets...but to fulfill" them. (Matthew 5:17).

Antonio Valeriano concludes the *Nican Mopohua* with, "No

person of this world had the privilege of painting such an image." This judgment, as embarrassing as it might sound to a rationalist mentality, has been corroborated over the course of the centuries as many painters, chemists, oculists, and photographers have examined the image. We can conclude by recalling the most recent of those studies, that of NASA engineer Philip S. Callaghan. With a cold and cautious tone, but no less categorical, he reiterated that same Indian opinion: "It proves

inexplicable for the current state of science."

Notes

1. de Sahagun, Fr. Bernardino. Historia General de las Cosas de la Nueva España, Editorial Porrúa, Colección "Sepan Cuantos." no. 300, México, 1975, Libro VI, cap. no. 23, p. 344.

2. "Testimonio Auténtico de las Informaciones sobre el Milagro de la Aparición. Recibidas el año de 1666". Published by P. Vera Hipólito, Amecameca, 1889. 2o. Testigo, 5a, Pregunta, p. 27.

CPSIA information can be obtained
at www.ICGtesting.com
Printed in the USA
BVHW042131211121
622208BV00013B/444